FLORIDA

POEMS

ALSO BY CAMPBELL McGRATH

Road Atlas

Spring Comes to Chicago

American Noise

Capitalism

FLORIDA POEMS

CAMPBELL McGRATH

An Imprint of HarperCollinsPublishers

HarperCollins books may be purchased for educational, business, or sales promotional use. For information please write: Special Markets Department, HarperCollins Publishers Inc., 10 East 53rd Street, New York, NY 10022.

First Ecco paperback edition 2003

Designed by Jessica Shatan

The Library of Congress has catalogued the hardcover edition as follows:

McGrath, Campbell, 1962–
  Florida Poems / Campbell McGrath.
    p. cm.
  ISBN 0-06-000896-2 (hardcover)
    1. Florida—Poetry. I. Title

  PS3563.C3658 F57 2002
  811'.54—dc21   2001040485

ISBN 0-06-052736-6 (pbk.)

03 04 05 06 07 ❖/QB 10 9 8 7 6 5 4 3 2

For Elizabeth

ACKNOWLEDGMENTS

With thanks to the editors of the publications in which the following poems have appeared:

"At the Royal Palm Barbershop," *Solo*.

"Because This Is Florida," "Hemingway Dines on Boiled Shrimp and Beer," and "Seashells, Manasota Key," *Paris Review*.

"Benediction for the Savior of Orlando," *Indiana Review*.

"Edison in Fort Myers, 1885," *Ploughshares*.

"Elizabeth Bishop in the House on White Street," "Mile Marker 73, Lower Matecumbe Key," and "The Strangler Fig," *Quarterly West*.

"Florida (Mangrovia)," "Maizel at Shorty's in Kendall," "The Florida Anasazi," and "The Florida Poem," *TriQuarterly*.

"Florida (Paradise)," *Sycamore Review*.

"The Miami Beach Holocaust Memorial," *Gettysburg Review*.

"The Zebra Longwing," *Kenyon Review*.

"Trouble with Miami," *Graffiti Rag*.

"William Bartram Beset by Crocodiles or Alligators," *Salt Hill*.

"Florida (Mangrovia)" and "The Florida Anasazi" were anthologized in *The New American Poets,* University Press of New England.
"The Manatee" and "The Miami Beach Holocaust Memorial" were anthologized in *Poets of the New Century,* David R. Godine Publishers.

Several of these poems appeared in *Mangrovia,* a limited edition chapbook from Short Line Editions, Saint Paul, Minnesota.

~

My thanks to Florida International University, to Kate and Kingsley Tufts and their executors at Claremont Graduate University, the Witter Bynner Foundation and Robert Pinsky, the John Simon Guggenheim Memorial Foundation, and the John D. and Catherine T. MacArthur Foundation for the support—an embarrassment of philanthropic riches—that enabled the timely completion of this book.

Among many debts of artistic gratitude, "A City in the Clouds" and "The Florida Poem" owe much, respectively, to Aristophanes and Pablo Neruda. "William Bartram Beset by Crocodiles or Alligators" is more theft than loan, having been adapted, bowdlerized, and otherwise plagiarized from William Bartram's inimitable *Travels.*

CONTENTS

THREE: THE FLORIDA POEM

ONE

FLORA & FAUNA

A City in the Clouds

1. The First Days

Nobody knew how the alligators had come to live in the clouds
but there they were, brutishly snarling and snapping
around the feet of the first, courageous citizens to embark,
at which point it was too late to do anything but smile
and learn to live with them, small concern at a moment
of such significance, in a world of such size and wonderment,
and anyway the alligators felt no urging toward companionship
and soon migrated spraddle-legged and bellowing
to the far outlying cloudlands and were seldom seen again
for many years, and anyway it was all smiles, or mostly,
in those first, halcyon, most splendid of days.

It was a time of solidarity and joy, a golden age
of amazement at their audacity and luck
when the tasks of managing a new life in the stratosphere
were mastered with harmonic grace and wisdom,
serenity absorbed by nimbus of star-fall or moon-rise
to gild them as obelisks on a miraculous plateau
and cast their shadows as laughing masks
against the corrugated damask of that realm.

Great works were undertaken: the drafting of laws,
the balancing of rights and obligations. Fields were planted.
The water-harvesting machinery was assembled
and turned on; cisterns and storage ponds filled slowly
but inexorably with unrained water, liquid measure
of the blessings of present fortune and future promise.

Communal edifices were surveyed and dedicated,
lyceum and civic center, an amphitheater for town meetings.
Flexible dwellings of thatch and mesh were woven,
simple but sturdy, in accordance with their needs,
terraces and plazas, spires and cupolas and palisades,
orchid gardens with rain-fountains hewn from the living mist
and cantilevered footpaths cast in gulf-straddling arcs
to accommodate the magisterial vista of the world below
and the spidering industry of construction above as
day after day, week after week, a city arose in the sky.

2. The Clouds

Times the clouds were like riven badlands, foils and arroyos and
    alluvial fans, rough country best traversed with safety ropes as if
    crossing polar seas over plates of tilting ice.

~

Times the clouds were umbels
or whale spouts,
fields of coreopsis, a vast mushroom farm.

~

Times the clouds lay smooth as a tabletop and children dangled their
    feet as if to fish from an old trestle bridge;
here too one might try his luck, over coastal waters of aquamarine or
    some green, bomb-sighted lake below,
though it took a great hoard of spooled line and a keen eye for
    trajectory and wind shear and then there was

the small matter of a fish
to be hauled into the sky!

~

Times the clouds were gongs and temples, a rapture in pewter, grand
    passions, coffers of incense and precious woods.

~

Times the clouds were battalions of tired oxen, cavalries of manta
   rays, schooled dolphins carving a wake in blue glass,

an army of animals or
a wide plain of chairs and pillows,
a soft-focus Serengeti,
a wilderness of distant billows.

A new land, a new sea.
A new world.

A city.

3. The Shapes and the Lines

From the clouds, looking down, it was clear
how little the shapes and the lines
really meant—sawtooth geometries of human industry
and political jurisdiction—and it was clear that where there was order
in the world it was the polymorphic order of nature:
imperious sweep of the coast, cut-line of the great bays like a knife
pressed into fresh dough, bights and coves, the sandy plume
of Cape Canaveral like an out-flexed thumb
to roil the current with its checkerboard of launching pads,
fields of eel grass against white sand, a coral reef
shaped as an Alexandrian seahorse,
cypress stands and cane breaks, lenticular hammocks,
the Everglades in flood like a puddled backyard of impossible
    dimension,
a camouflage sheet of olive and brown or a painter's riddle
of figure and background. And where
there was chaos
it was graven in strokes of righteous angularity:
bolus of a city inscribed by giant needles,
nexus of highways, tangle of vectors on crumpled papyrus,
power lines across the pine forest, fate line
engraved in the lithosphere
of the palm,
tributary, vesicle, arterial etching,
gyres and demilunes of irrigation, feeder patterns
and data fields and tables
of elements,
a circumstantial sociology of visual stimuli they knew,
as exiles, to signify less

than the sum of its parts, a world of
surfaces,
light and shadow,
a world of images and symbols, binary strings
of weeds and crops, ones
and zeroes,
citrus groves a sequence of in-stepped rectangles
like mass graves hurriedly filled,
insular obloids signifying sloughs and sinks,
unwanted earth, undrainable terrain,
odd-lot trinkets
and jigsaw curios like a necklace of charms
spilled across the lunch counter—
baseball diamonds,
salt works, phosphate mines, a horse track.
The only border that mattered more
than the one between the realms of man and nature
was the gulf that separated them from both
and freed them from the earth's attendant concerns,
or so they hoped and believed, as they believed the clouds
they lived and prospered in to be self-reliant,
though a meteorologist might question their science,
and a philosopher might wonder at the sight of their shadow
thrown down again and again upon the terrestrial
regime like a doppelganger or rain
or a reign of ether, the negative of the film
their lives were creating in the camera obscura of midair.

4. The Fruits of the Earth

They missed things, various places and objects, old friends or distant
    cousins, specific sounds, familiar certainties.

Of course, it was inevitable, it had been planned for, though none had
    anticipated the severity of their longings
or knew if these were due to pangs of separation or unpaid claims of
    the planet upon their bodies
or because the clouds with their misty distances and imprecise edges
    were truly nostalgia's kingdom.

Shoes, for instance, of which
there was no need in that cushioned world.

And food.

It was nourishing but dull to subsist on shrimp and wild birds' eggs
    when flavors as rich and diverse as butterflies
danced in their memories like the chords of a lullaby. Certainly their
    fields were fertile when tended thoughtfully—
and gorgeous, of a dawn, apportioned with egrets catching blue fire as
    a chalice might brim with jeweled light—
and the hydroponic tents yielded bumper crops of legumes and
    vegetables, but fruit remained a problem.

Trees would not take root in the uncertain footing of the cloudbanks,
    and the orchards of seedlings they had planted failed,
and they yearned for the sensuous tastes to which they had been
    accustomed, skin and flesh, the opulent nectar.

Thus commenced the ritual of trade
between earth and sky.

Their original system of lifts and pulleys had proven naively
    inadequate, and now the first of the pipelines was constructed
to carry the harvested water earthward, and the freight elevator with
    its midair landings and maintenance decks
began its steady vertical pilgrimage bearing crates of tangerines and
    oranges, peaches and mangoes,
whatever could be gathered at the ever-shifting terminal point where
    the wind-flexed elevator shaft met the ground.

One day, as a joke—malicious or whimsical none can say—the cargo
    loaders sent up some food from McDonald's,
and there was much laughter and merriment among those who lived
    in the clouds, laughter as well as surprise,
for they were astonished at how vividly they remembered it all, the
    thin embossed napkins and red-and-yellow-striped straws,
the sugary hamburger buns and salty ketchup, the wilted french fries
    so good when just made—they remembered it

and they missed it!

The young most clearly of all remembered, and they danced and
    clapped with joyful abandon throughout the day,
and later that evening in the light of the cold, true constellations the
    citizens assembled to confer in their amphitheater

and it was decided that this thread of connection with their past was a
   good thing, though some decried it,
and as there was a need for rituals in their airy community, to thicken
   the weave of its social fabric,
it was decided they would partake of a common supper on the last
   Sunday of every month, as on that first Sunday,

and so began the Feast of the Happy Meals.

5. The Birds

Not songbirds, particularly, but marsh birds and stalking birds,
the many species of storks, egrets, bitterns, night herons,
oceangoing gulls and petrels, squadrons of pelicans,
flocks of grackles and raucous green parrots,
kingfishers, jays, ravens, mockingbirds, geese and ducks,
a great many raptors, kestrels and ospreys and red-tailed hawks,
an occasional eagle, black rings of buzzards or turkey vultures
materializing like Wagnerian wraiths from below.

In that high, empyrean place the birds were their brothers,
their friends and lone companions—except
for the misbegotten and all-but-forgotten alligators—
and from the first there were many who worshiped them,
and many who were angered by their depredations.
Rice fields pillaged by crows or mallards,
starlings spoiling freshly threshed grain,
egrets thieving shrimp from the aquaculture ponds.
They did what little they could to protect their crops,
scarecrows and firecrackers, swathes of protective netting,
but here the terrain was malleable and ever-shifting,
and the birds slipped past the sliding margins,
or squeezed through the cushiony, sponge-wet mist.
Wisest of the fish stealers, the great blue herons
soon learned to fly straight into the clouds and hide there,
banqueting right through the bottoms of the ponds!

It was a divisive time for the citizens of the clouds,
though it was neither the first nor last crisis to confront them.
Difficult choices needed to be made, and in the end,

after long and bitter debate, it was determined that the best
of the limited options available to them was guns.
Guns! The decision was greeted with acrimony.
There were demonstrations. There were denunciations
which were answered with official pronouncements.
The guns would be imported in limited numbers,
to be used only by specially appointed game wardens;
the killing of the birds was not a campaign of extermination
but a defensive action, a terrible but unavoidable
measure intended to secure their limited resources,
a culling of the flocks, a harvest of sorts, a project
whose success might well have unforeseen positive
repercussions in the long run for their avian friends.

There were more marches, louder and angrier.
There were acts of civil disobedience, acts of destruction
immediately labeled by the authorities as sabotage.
There were—here the official language must be employed—
provocations that could not in good conscience be ignored,
and as soon as the civic center had been retrofitted
with bars and cells it filled quickly with the jailed
supporters of the birds, widely condemned not as terrorists
but deluded and not altogether unsympathetic extremists,
called Egrets or Skraelings or simply the Bird People.

The idea of a prison in the clouds ran contrary
to everything the citizens had hoped for and believed
about themselves and their society and yet
as a temporary measure in troubled times it was tolerated

if not condoned. Still, it was the will of the people
that an amnesty be declared, which it was,
though the fissures that had opened among them
would not prove to be easily bridged.

Soon after their release, the Bird People moved
away from the city in the clouds altogether
to establish rough settlements of open huts in the wastes,
dressing in mist and heron feathers, plumbing
the interiors of the towering seasonal thunderheads
to catch the spark of lightning for the cloud-lanterns
in their lighthouses, until in time even their lighthouse
beacons were glimpsed less and less often
and were at last dismissed as atmospheric anomalies,
until the Bird People came to be thought of as
sacred predecessors, mythic creatures who would never
have deigned reside in any mere human city,
ancestral beings of the upper atmosphere.

6. The Machines

There were problems with the machines.

Few in the clouds knew anymore how to care for them—the giant
    evaporators and mist harvesters,
the piston-driven reapers and solar distillation panels—and new parts
    were obtainable only at great expense from below,
a cost that seemed unwise or insupportable to many, and so began the
    transition to manual cultivation.

The work was not easy: obdurate sunlight, aching muscles, heatstroke
    and vertigo as the clouds heaved and shifted.
Laborers were needed in larger numbers than ever before to build
    dikes and scuppers, retaining walls and entrapment ponds,
to herd the clouds as needed into the vapor paddies and drying tents
    with fat brooms and scooplike paddles,
to man the pumps for the earthward flow of water upon which their
    entire economy depended.

The question that confronted them, in that era of plenty, when there
    was yet much work to be done,
was how to apportion the tasks, now that the old methods of day
    labor and individual choice no longer sufficed.
And how to account for the changes that had overcome them in
    regards to their willingness to toil in the fields
and their eagerness to enjoy the fruits of that labor, with so many new
    and enticing fruits to be enjoyed.

The cultivation of orchids had long been their practice, for of all
    creatures orchids had proven beloved of the clouds
and flourished in their sphagnum-soft folds and crevices, proliferating
    and mutating into ever more protean and exotic varieties,
seeming, at times, to hang suspended as luxurious waterfalls rooted in
    the barest mist or veil of vapor,
their night-perfumes of sufficient potency to summon a
    phantasmagoria of moths from the land below,

but now the flowers themselves became secondary to the speculation
    in seed futures and the numerological orchid lotteries,
a translation of the thing into the ghost of the thing, as their lives in
    the clouds so often seemed a spectral transliteration
of some previous estate, rarefied version of a bygone text whose key
    they saw encoded within the figurations of their games of chance,
all forms of luck held sacred as versions of the blind celestial life-
    force, thunderbolt or gamut of random, originating cosmic energy.

At long last, too, the clouds were plugged into the television cable,
    with premium channels provided free to all subscribers—
immense new billboards for Disney Channel and HBO had been
    slung and fastened to the underbelly of the clouds
alongside the original flashing golden arches with their fat snake of
    power cables writhing earthward—
and the first of three specially customized McDonald's slated to grace
    their city was already well under construction.

In that moment began the public debates that ended with the
  resolution to open the clouds to new settlement.

From the first, there had been many back on earth desirous of coming
  to live amongst the citizens in the sky,
and for years small planes had been found, crash-landed in the cloud-
  wastes, and the debris of homemade balloons,
on which families had journeyed to their ethereal world, slipping
  silently into the margins of society.
Now it was decided that legal immigration should commence, with
  those who arrived assigned specific labor
in agriculture or support services, in the fields or at the water pumps,
  at the health spas or the new casino,
work they performed with great vigor and happiness, looking forward
  to the day of their eventual emancipation,

a freedom earned with honest industry,
a freedom which receded elusively before them,

until the workers began to wonder at the conditions of their
  detainment, year after year, which was only just and reasonable.

7. The Slaves

Indeed there was much work to be done in the clouds, indisputably so, and thus there must be workers, yes, surely, and yet, between the much and the many, the few and the little, the doing and the not-doing, yawned a great chasm of possibility. Why should all be compelled to work, when the many might work more, leaving the few to enjoy the rewards of that common labor for the rest? But who among them would choose to work, it was wondered aloud, while others remained at leisure? Why not the newcomers, such robust and tireless helpers? But already the newcomers were agitating for their freedom, small wonder, and on what grounds could it be denied them in perpetuity? Great accomplishments demand great sacrifices, my friends, my fellow citizens. Athens, without its helots, would have raised no Acropolis, produced no Pericles or Plato, and Rome was not built without the breaking of eggs, which after all is the way of nature. Is not the honey bee content to labor for its queen? Are not the ants united in their toil for the colony, united in blind obedience, willing drones, eager vassals, happy slaves? That long, hollow, terrible syllable: slaves. And now it was there among them, as a party to be reckoned with, for what had once been uttered could not be unsaid. But it was against their laws and charters, it violated their mandate against discrimination! What if it were nondiscriminatory? What if everyone became a slave, all the newcomers, regardless of race, religion, age or creed? What if it were not a publicly acknowledged servitude but a furtive one, a tacit one? What if the slaves themselves submitted to their condition in return for certain promises, for food and housing, reasonable wages, goods and properties—there was plenty for all in their society and why not grant them a healthy share in that plenty so long as their work was accomplished, why not enjoin that very plenty as tool of their acquiescence? But surely it will not suffice to offer material goods, not even great wealth, for they will recognize their enslavement and rebel against it. What if there were other enticements, promises of material amelioration and generational advancement, a system that offered the hope of emancipation without need of providing it, for hope would be enough, the hope of transcendence, the hope of fulfillment, and as the years passed even these concessions might be withdrawn, as those born to the system no longer wondered at its mechanisms, and the bonds that held them were deemed inevitable, for there would be no repeat of history's errors, no captives carried in chains, no sale or sign of ownership, for it would be systemic, it would be societal, it would be communal? A pause now, a ripening. It was possible, yes, if they themselves consented to it, if there was a contract of some kind, an agreement entered into, a compact. Or an oath of citizenship? Or a pledge of allegiance?

8. The Alligators

Not the fall of a single sparrow, not the loss of a single feather, no life
    was too humble to merit the concern
of that society founded in utopian fellowship in the sky, and so when
    the alligators began to prey on the slaves
sent out each morning to the fields and greenhouses and orchid
    pavilions strewn across the cloudplains,
and to the aquaculture ponds pushed farther and farther away from
    the ever-enlarging city, something had to be done.

Alligators! In the clouds?
But where had they come from, how—?

Though some said they had always been there, even on the first day, at
    the first footfall, few remembered or cared to try;
what mattered was that they were here now, and the time had come to
    deal with them, once and for all.

Along the perimeter of cultivation fences went up, barbed wire strung
    right through the soft matter of the clouds,
watchtowers and surveillance equipment, warning sirens, blinds for
    the hunters to await their slow-moving quarry.
The school, having long since fallen into disuse, became an armory for
    the array of weapons that would be needed;
the political prisoners and detainees were moved from their cells to a
    series of hastily built work camps,
freeing the former civic center to become the barracks for those
    involved in the alligator-eradication program.

It was a time of fear and rumors.

What about the strange night-flashes in the clouds, the ominous
    signals that some said were lighthouses?
What about the feathered people claimed to walk like mist giants
    there, might not they be harboring the alligators,

aiding and abetting their misdeeds?

In this way were the Bird People rediscovered by the city in the
    clouds, and made fugitives,
and while many fled once and for all back to earth, climbing at great
    peril down rope ladders to the Florida Keys,
many chose to remain in the sky where they were hunted down and
    incarcerated, and in their hunting were committed certain acts of
    excess,

though the word "atrocity" was deemed legally inadmissible when the
    Tribunal for Truth and Reconciliation
convened to consider the appeals for official acknowledgment and the
    civil suits brought by the families of the victims
against certain notorious members of the Security Forces—but no
    matter how many alligators the hunters killed and flayed

there seemed to be no end to them.

The decision was made to redouble their efforts not merely at
    prosecuting the war against these primordial foes

but at denying them refuge in the reefs and archipelagoes and the high
   cirrus plains that were their home.
The rate of the moisture harvest was ratcheted upward, then up again,
   creating in the process a windfall of income for the city
which had nonetheless slipped so deeply into debt that the first of the
   big casino-hotel projects was soon followed by others—

Thunderdome, Cloudiana, the MGM Valhalla—

and a series of time-share resort developments were granted zoning
   variances in anticipation of much-needed tax revenues,
while talk of a ballyhooed Disneyland was quickly shelved—not even
   the Imagineers could support such a structure in the sky!

New evaporation technologies were developed; vast cohorts of
   additional immigrants were admitted and put to work.

The machines came back on.

Their delicate solar mechanisms and wind-throttled engines could no
   longer be repaired, of course,
and so an antiquated electrical plant was imported and reassembled to
   power the pumps directly,
and though the smoke cast a dreadful pall in the crystalline air that
   had been their pride and glory
and stained the clouds with a watery tonic of boot-grey ashes it was
   deemed a success when the hunters reported

that outlying cloudlands
had at last begun to dry up and disappear—

few had seen for themselves this remarkable sign of transformation for
    few of the citizens left their homes anymore,
fearing the ill effects of poisoned air and endemic street crime—
    children had been abducted, more would soon vanish—

and the alligators were now so densely concentrated in their
    sanctuaries that it was thought to be a matter of weeks at most
until the last of them would have been dispatched and things at last
    could return to the way they had been in the time before,
or the time before that, or even, if any still recalled it, the time before
    the time before the time before that.

9. The Clouds

Times the clouds were like chisel-strokes in amber, flocks of anvils,
   valleys of kings, a forest of statues or disfigured pillars.

~

Times the clouds were gouged and tined by tooth-marks of a vast
   unseen devourer as if rude hills scraped to the bone.

~

Times the clouds were cairns or dolmen,
     a wind-bent cromlech
     of zoomorphic ivory,
apocryphal glyphs from a lipogramatic lexicon,
     ashen lamentations,
     a threnody of broken vowels,
petals of wild roses in a lidless cinerarium.

~

Times the clouds were lit with distant fire and rumbled all night with
   the death-cries of the alligators
and the pop-pop of the hunters' rifles and their jubilant calls
   harmonizing with the wails of the sirens
as the littered wrappers of Filet-O-Fish sandwiches battened in the
   barbed wire to glimmer in the searchlights

like tiles of a lost mosaic
or wild ghostly facets of a jewel.

10. The Last Days

The last days of the city in the clouds were in many ways
like those that had gone before: each morning
the sun arose from beneath them
in a corona of atmospheric fire; each night
it slipped beneath the velvet omphalos of their horizon.

But as the raw and fragile tissue of the clouds
was sucked into the maw of the unresting pumps
not only did the outlying regions diminish
but the fundamental clouds of the city grew ever thinner,
and as they thinned they rose to a greater height,
and the cold wind of the jetstream assailed them
in their latticed dwellings built for gentler climes.

Things were lost: bottles, alarm clocks, cases of rifle shells.

Things slipped through the clouds and fell, and yes,
the slaves were now roped together in work gangs,
so that any who tumbled through might be safely retrieved,
but the war against the alligators was deemed
so vital to their interests that any means to victory
was defensible, and anyway the citizens did not welcome
the complaints of their neighbors from below,
who seemed to them merely envious,
while to the earth dwellers the city in the clouds,
when they thought of it at all, seemed a nuisance and an eyesore,
with its web of cables and power couplings,
its leaking sewers and fleets of chartered casino buses,
its bleak death-mask etched in soot,

its garish and ever-expanding array of advertisements—
Nike was now the official footwear of the clouds;
Microsoft its software—like a vast, pulsating, flat-panel blimp.

From the ground it was apparent what was about to happen,
as the city's foundations grew starkly exposed,
but they said nothing to those who anyway had no ears
to hear them and no eyes to see the warnings

etched against the sky.

The last night, as always, the moon
from among the wheeling stars cast down its unfiltered gaze
onto the great sky-prairie,
a place at last subdued, defeated, bereft
of all but the thin shrouds and tattered shreds of cloud
upon which the city perched.

The hunters were asleep in their barracks,
the slaves at rest in their tenements,
the citizens slumbered in ignorance of their fate,

so it was that none were awake to witness that instant—

none but the sentries in their silent watchtowers
and the never-resting croupiers and blackjack dealers
and the early crew brewing coffee for the morning rush—

when the minarets shook and the spires wobbled
as the great pumps sucked in their final breath of vapor
and the machines ground to a halt
and the last filament of cloud was processed into liquid water
which, having no longer any surface on which to rest,

fell to the ground as a soft rain

while the city fell as ruins
of great beauty

but little value save as a photo opportunity
for the trickle of tourists
who for a brief while came to view them,
then quickly scavenged, sold for scrap, paved over,
grown over by the jungled foliage,
and so lost without a trace,
erased forever from human memory,

though not from the dim, enduring minds
of its only survivors, the alligators
who splashed down across the state of Florida
in swamps and water hazards and backyard swimming pools,
haunted through all the lonely days of their existence
by a vision of lost glory,
and a desire for blood vengeance,
and a particular, unquenchable, marrow-racking sorrow,

a grief known only to those who,
having once been granted license to a world of airy splendor
must abide in the compromised mud of their downfall,
dreaming up at the heavens,
awaiting the hour of their restitution.

TWO

FLORIDIANA

Florida

Paradise must resemble this realm of clouds, birds and flowers!

Red woodpecker in the royal palm: so too in that forum shall trees
    uphold the firmament!

Mockingbird in the neighbor's garden, wild green parrot in the
    grapefruit tree:
twisted of years, stretching its scaly neck across the hedge,
strange to know this branch has grown precisely thus to yield its
    shapely fruit unto my hand!

So shall the limbs of that eternal orchard be laden!

Hibiscus, ixora, alamanda, oleander: so shall every flower be given
    voice!

There too, below, the billows of the sea: above, the reefs of dawn and
    sunset,
thunderheads risen like the fists of immortals,
celestial cumulus like the bearers of something immense held dangling.

Perfume of jasmine, egret in moonlight, trade wind through the
    jacaranda: nor night shall mask their glory,

nor darkness still the turmoil of our senses.

The Orange

Gone to swim after walking the boys to school.
Overcast morning, midweek, off-season,
few souls to brave the warm, storm-tossed waves,
not wild but rough for this tranquil coast.

Swimming now. In rhythm, arm over arm,
let the ocean buoy the body and the legs work little,
wave overhead, crash and roll with it, breathe,
stretch and build, windmill, climb the foam. Breathe,

breathe. Traveling downwind I make good time
and spot the marker by which I know to halt
and forge my way ashore. Who am I
to question the current? Surely this is peace abiding.

Walking back along the beach I mark the signs of erosion,
bide the usual flotsam of seagrass and fan coral,
a float from somebody's fishing boat,
crusted with sponge and barnacles, and then I find

the orange. Single irradiant sphere on the sand,
tide-washed, glistening as if new born,
golden orb, miraculous ur-fruit,
in all that sweep of horizon the only point of color.

Cross-legged on my towel I let the juice course
and mingle with the film of salt on my lips
and the sand in my beard as I steadily peel and eat it.
Considering the ancient lineage of this fruit,

the long history of its dispersal around the globe
on currents of animal and human migration,
and in light of the importance of the citrus industry
to the state of Florida, I will not claim

it was the best and sweetest orange in the world,
though it was, o great salt water
of eternity,
o strange and bountiful orchard.

The Key Lime

Curiously yellow hand-grenade
of flavor; Molotov cocktail
for a revolution against the bland.

Because This Is Florida

Because this is Florida, we can be what we choose to be,
say, Dixie-fried Cubano rednecks. It's that kind of place.
When the heavy metal band plays "Rocky Top, Tennessee"

they all stomp and sing along—I should say *we*
sing along, at the annual State Fair, a very weird place.
Because this is Florida, I feel like an anomaly,

but the truth of it is I'm them and they're me,
and now we're stamping and hooting all over the place
while the Texas swing band plays "Rocky Top, Tennessee"

and Haitian kids dip kettle candy beneath a live oak tree
in historic *Cracker Country,* apt and ironic misnomer for the place,
because this is Florida, after all, not Texas or Tennessee.

Florida, Florida. At times I can't believe what I see
and don't know how to feel about living in a place
where a bluegrass fiddler plays "Rocky Top, Tennessee"

while Rome burns. Is it just me, or an epidemic of mistaken identity,
the state of confusion that plagues this sun-bedeviled place?
Because this is Florida, I beg you to believe me,
the steel drum band from Trinidad plays "Rocky Top, Tennessee."

William Bartram Beset by Crocodiles or Alligators

How shall I Express myself so as to convey an Adequate Idea of it to
the Reader, and yet avoid raising Suspicions of my Veracity?

How happily situated is this retired Spot of Earth!
What an Elysium it is!
Where the wandering Siminole, the naked red Warrior, Roams at
Large,
And after the Vigorous Chase retires from the scorching Heat of the
meridian Sun.
Here he reclines, and reposes under the Odoriferous Shades of
Zanthoxylon, his verdant Couch guarded by the Deity;
Liberty, and the Muses, inspiring him with Wisdom and Valour,
Whilst the Balmy Zephyrs fan him to Sleep.

Behold, for instance, a Vast Circular Expanse before you, Waters so
extremely clear as to be absolutely Diaphanos or Transparent as the
Aether;
The Margin of the basin ornamented with a great Variety of fruitful
and floriferous Trees, Shrubs, and Plants,
The pendant golden Orange dancing on the Surface of the Pellucid
Waters,
Air vibrating with Melody of the Merry Birds,
The aromatic Grove,
Balmy Lantana, ambrosial Citra, perfumed Crinum,
Protected by encircling Ranks of Yucca gloriosa.

At the same instant, innumerable Bands of Fish are seen: the
devouring Garfish, inimical Trout, and all the varieties of gilded
painted Bream;

The barbed Catfish, dreaded Sting-Ray, Skate, and Flounder,
Spotted Bass, Sheeps Head and ominous Drum.
Behold yet some Thing far more admirable!
See whole Armies descending
Into an Abyss, into the mouth of the bubbling Fountain: they disappear!
Are they gone Forever?
I raise my eyes with Terror and Astonishment,
When behold them Emerging as from the Blue of Another World,
Apparently at a vast Distance; no bigger than Flies or Minnows,
    gradually enlarging, brilliant Colors painting the Fluid.
Now they come forward Rapidly, with the elastic expanding Column
    of crystalline Waters,
Suffering themselves to be gently Lifted or Borne up, like Butterflies;
Once more they Descend, diverge, move off; when they rally, Form
    Again, and rejoin their kindred Tribes.
There seems no Medium; you imagine the Picture to be within Inches
    of your Gaze, that you may reach out
And touch any of these Fish, when they are Twenty or Thirty Feet
    distant,
Or put your Finger upon the Crocodile's Eye,
For here too is that Voracious Creature, the Alligator or Crocodile,
Stretched along at Full Length, as the trunk of a Tree in Size, its Head,
    at a Distance, resembling a great Chunk of Wood floating about.
When full grown it is a Very Large and Terrible Creature, and of
    prodigious Strength, Activity and Swiftness in the water.
Its body is Large as that of a Horse; its Shape exactly resembles a Lizard,
Except the Tail, which is Flat or Cuneiform,
Gradually diminishing from the Abdomen to the Extremity, which,
    with the Whole Body, is covered with Horny Plates or Squammae.

It was by this time after Noon.

Surfeited by enchantments, I nonetheless saw fit to Depart the Spring,
   of a type Most Prevalent in these parts,
Returning toward the Landing and my Bark, for purpose of mounting
   Higher up the River before Night fall,
Crossing again a Landscape Unparalleled, as I think, Green Fields
Interspersed with Hommocks or Islets of Trees, where the Magnolia
   and Lordly Palm stand conspicuous.
Bounteous Kingdom of Flora!
What a beautiful Display of Vegetation is before me!
How the Dew-drops Twinkle and play upon the Sight, trembling on
   the Tips of the Lucid, Green Savanna,
As the Gem that Flames on the Turban of the Eastern Prince.
See the pearly Tears rolling off the Buds of the expanding Granadilla;
Behold the azure Fields of cerulean Ixea!
What can equal the rich golden Flowers of the Canna lutea which
   Ornament the Banks of yon serpentine Rivulet;
The gay Phlox, associated with the purple Verben corymbosa,
Pearly Gnaphalium, and silvery Perdicium?
How fantastical looks the libertine Clitoria, mantling the Vistas!

Such was the country thereabouts, traversed N. westerly to the
   Riverbank.

Evening rapidly approaching, the Alligators
Began to Roar and Appear in uncommon Numbers along the Shore
And in the Water as I put forth,

Furnishing myself with a Stout Club for my Defense.

I concluded to be Expeditious in my Journey,

Being Conscious of some Danger and Difficulty, yet could not help to
Notice

That Here is in this River, and in the Waters all over Florida,

A very Curious and Handsome Species of Birds,

The people call them Snake Birds; I think I have seen Paintings of
them on Chinese screens and other India Pictures:

They seem to be a species of Cormorant or Loon, but Far more
Beautiful.

I doubt not but if this Bird had been an Inhabitant of the Tiber in
Ovid's day,

It would have furnished him with a Subject for some Lovely and
Entertaining Metamorphoses.

I believe it Feeds Intirely on Fish, for its Flesh smells and tastes
Strong of it;

It is scarcely to be Eaten, Unless constrained by intolerable Hunger.

Passing along the Shoal Banks, towards a type of Cove or Lagoon, the
River grew narrowed and Crowded shore to shore with Crocodiles,

Feeding apparently on the great Quantities of Fish in those Straits.

Despite my wish to augment my Collections with several of the admirably
beautiful and singular Specimens along this Stretch of River,

Many of them new to me, and to Science,

I determined to Desist from such efforts under the present
Predicament,

Marveling at the laughing Coots with wings half spread Tripping over
the little wavelets;

The Verges elegantly Embellished with flowering Plants, floating
     Lawns of the Pistia and Nymphea;
Young Broods of the painted summer Teal skimming the still Surface
     of the Waters, Unconscious of Danger,
Frequently Surprised by the voracious Trout; and he, in Turn,
By the Subtle Greedy Alligator.

Behold him rushing forth from the Flags and Reeds!
His enormous Body swells!
His plaited Tail brandished high, floats upon the Lake!
The Waters like a Cataract descend from his opening Jawes!
Clouds of Smoke issue from his Dilated Nostrils!
The Earth trembles with his Thunder!

My Apprehensions were Highly Alarmed.

Paddling with all my Might I made towards the Entrance of the
     Lagoon, hoping to be Sheltered from the Multitude of my Assailants,
But ere I had Half-Way reached the Place I was Attacked on all Sides.
My situation now became Precarious to the last Degree: two very
     Large Ones assailed me at close quarters,
Roaring terribly and belching Floods of Water over me.
They struck their Jawes together so near to my Ears,
As almost to Stun Me, and I expected
Any Minute to be dragged out of the Boat and Instantly Devoured.
Then it was I applied my Weapon so Effectually, Though at Random,
     as to Beat them off a Little.

I made for the Shore, as the only Means Left for my preservation,
Sure the Crocodiles designed to Renew the Battle,
When they suddenly Dart upon Each Other, and a Terrific Conflict
    ensues.
The boiling Surface of the Lake marks their rapid Course, as they now
    Sink to the Bottom folded together in Horrid Wreaths.
Again they rise, their Jawes clap together.
Again they sink, when the Contest ends at the Muddy Bottom,
And the Vanquished makes a hazardous Escape, hiding in the
    turbulent Waters and Sedge.
The proud Victor exults, Shores and deep surrounding Forests re-
    echoing his Dreadful Roar,
Together with the triumphing Shouts of the plaited Tribes around,
    Witnesses of the Combat.

Evening coming on Apace, I began to look out for High Land to
    encamp upon, being Surrounded by Swamps and Marshes on both
    Sides of me.
It was some Time before I found a tolerably suitable Place, with Yet
    Great Numbers of Crocodiles in sight on both Shores.
When I landed it was quite Dark; and in collecting Wood for my Fire,
    strolling about the Groves,
I found the Surface of the Ground very uneven,
By means of little Mounts and Ridges;
I had taken up my Lodging on the border of an Ancient Burying-
    Ground,
Containing Sepulchres or Tumuli of the Yamasees,

Now overgrown with Orange trees, Live Oaks, Laurel Magnolias, Red
    Bays and other Trees and shrubs,
Who were here slain by the Creeks in the Last Decisive Battle,
The Creeks having driven them into this Point, between the doubling
    of the River, where few of them escaped the Fury of their
    conquerors.

These Graves occupied the whole grove,
Some Two or Three Acres.

As for Provisions, I had saved one or two barbecued Trout, somewhat
    Injured by the Sun and Heat of the Day;
Yet by Stewing them up with the Juice of Oranges, they served well
    Enough for my Supper, as I had by this time Little Relish for my
    Victuals,
For Constant Watching against the Attacks of Alligators, stinging of
    Musquitoes, and sultry Vapors,
Together with the Fatigues of working my Bark,
Had almost deprived me of Every Desire but that of ending my
    Troubles as speedily as possible.

All now Silent and Peaceable, I suddenly fell Asleep.

At Midnight I awake; when, Raising my head erect, I find myself
    Alone in the Wilderness of Florida.

Edison in Fort Myers, 1885

He was, in those years, the wizard of the place,
the state's most famous seasonal resident,
primordial snowbird, genius of machinery in a kingdom
whose vegetable dynamos outpulsed anything
even his well-greased corporate laboratories might envision,
imperator of science swathed in green, cocooned
in jungle xylem, this man who would bring light
into the darkness of civilization. *The first step
is an intuition, and comes with a burst,*
he offered in explanation of his repetitious genius,
and so it was with this place—Florida!—filament
sparking incandescent within the glassy belljar
of his cranium. Sailed up from the gulf on a whim
and bought his swath of land at a bend
in the big, irksome, manatee-laden river that very day,
though the place was nothing but cowboys and Indians then;
so named the estate he built Seminole Lodge
in honor of the natives who came still to trade in alligator
hides or sheathings of quill birds, or in memory
of the surrender of Chief Billy Bowlegs at this very spot
some forty years earlier. It was not, after all, Port Myers
but Fort Myers, relic of another militarized
episode of frontier diplomacy, localized generator
for the transmission of raw political power.
For Edison it was Eden along the Caloosahatchee,
and they still flock in droves to its lush abundance
from the small cold towns of Michigan and Ohio
that were his homeland, as moths must once have swarmed
the only electric light within a thousand miles

glimmering in the windows of his generator-fed workshop.
How many years of his life had he exchanged
for the name of that element with the strength and willingness
to burn? The secret of his success was
systematization. *All parts of the system must be
constructed with reference to all other parts.*
Thus when he came to plant his manorial gardens
it was a grand campaign of strategic engineering
with nothing left to chance hand or native grace,
grade and pitch and precise coordinates keyed
for each of nearly two thousand varieties of flowers
to be fertilized with imported guano, mulched and battened
beneath cotton cloth soaked in boiled linseed oil.
A nut fancier, he called for acres of peanuts, orchards
of English walnuts, pecans from Jacksonville, Brazil nuts,
filberts, soft-shell almonds. He shipped a thousand
pineapple plants from Key Largo; gooseberry bushes
imported from Spain; bramble patches of red and black
raspberries; cotton and tobacco; double rows of sugarcane.
Multitudes of fruit trees: banana, mango, guava,
peach, plum, pomegranate, alligator pear, grapefruit,
cherry, mulberry, crabapple, sapodilla and several
types of orange, including blood and mandarin.
Years later, in his eighties, he planted every species
of latex-bearing plant he could uncover and procure—
including hectares of goldenrod and a seedling ficus tree
brought from India by Henry Ford—in a patriotic quest
to isolate a domestic source of rubber, a last inventive
race he led for a glorious moment but lost by a nose

to the angel of death, though not before taking
his spring-training cuts with the Philadelphia Athletics
and hosting President-elect Herbert Hoover
on a triumphal open-car procession while
the Fort Myers Vocal Chorus sang "I Can't Give You
Anything But Love, Baby." It was 1929. The bells
of the Depression were tolling and his phonograph
business was finished, brought to its knees by radio.
Two years later the great man himself was dead.
The last thing he planted, the ficus carried home
by Ford in tribute to his Promethean friend and neighbor,
is today the largest tree in the state of Florida.

Florida

There is no hope of victory in this garden.
Bent to the lawn, I acknowledge defeat
in every blade of St. Augustine
grass destroyed by intractable cinchbugs.

Hours on end I pull the woody roots
of dollar weed from the soil. At night I dream
of vegetable genocide, so deep, so abiding,
has my hatred for that kingdom grown.

Near dawn I hear the scuttle of fruit rats
returning to their nest within our wall;
they walk the tightrope of the phone wires at dusk,
leap like acrobats into limbs of heavy citrus.

Something larger inhabits the crawlspace,
raccoon or opossum, purple carapace
of the landcrab emerging from its burrow.
On a branch, green caterpillars thick as a finger,

from which will rise some terrible nightmoth.
The snails leave calcified notice of their trespass;
in the rain they climb the hibiscus and wait.
I labor in sunlight, praying for stalemate.

Benediction for the Savior of Orlando

Signs and wonders: *Jesus Is Lord Over Greater Orlando*
snake-tagged in cadmium on a vine-grown cyclone
fence along I-4 southbound north of downtown
is a credo that subverts the conventional wisdom
that Walt Disney is the messiah and his minions the christened
stewards of this place, that the Kingdom to Come shall be Mickey's,
that the bread of our communion will be proffered by A.T.M.
and the wine quaffed without taint of sulfites
or trademark infringement, all of which is certainly true
and yet too pat, too much like shooting mice in a barrel
when there are nastier vermin to contest
and purgatories far worse than Disney's realm of immortal
simulacra suckled at the breast of Lake Buena Vista.
There is, for one, Orlando itself,
Orlando rightly considered, Orlando qua Orlando.
Nobody, anywhere, could honestly propose Orlando
as a fit model for human habitation,
city with the character of a turnpike restroom,
city with the soul of a fast-food establishment,
sanitized and corporatized, homogenous and formulaic.
Orlando is the holy land of the branded and franchised,
Orlando is the Jerusalem of commodified delight,
Orlando, Orlando, so many Orlandos
I commence to feel downright Shakespearean,
but here is no Rosalind to dignify our tale,
no Touchstone to transform its tragedy to farce,
because Orlando is the Florida I fear to conceive,
Florida ordained like the ante-chamber to that afterworld

where jackal-headed Anubis prepares his embalmer's instruments
to pump our veins with tincture of liquid sunshine
until we are reduced to somnambulant acquiescence,
a citizenry mummified within the cambric of material satiety,
within the gated stucco walls of economic segregation
and the hairy stucco arms of Armed Response security,
a people determined to rev our outboards and troll for bass
in the shadow of the form-glass temples to corporate profit
while the fill ponds grow heavy with duckweed and algae
and the golf courses burn with viridian fire
through seasons of rain and seasons of drought
and the metropolis spreads ever outward the bland picnic blankets
of its asphalt dominion, landscape drained of spontaneity and glee,
bones boiled free of communal gristle—is it any wonder
the children of this America rise up with guns
to wreak a senseless vengeance,
the very children that might have saved us,
the ones we had relied on to assemble in fellowship
and attend to councils of greater wisdom
than those to which we have given credence?
Perhaps the children were absent from school
the day these lessons were offered or perhaps
the lessons have been censored from the curriculum
or there was no curriculum or the schools
had been demolished to make room for the future,
a serial cataclysm of vinyl and asphalt,
a republic of bananas and Banana Republics,
where cars are the chosen and credit cards the elect,
where Judge Judy balances the Scales of Justice

and the anthem of our freedom is sung by Chuck E. Cheese.
Here I may testify with absolute conviction:
Chuck E. Cheese is the monstrous embodiment of a nightmare,
the bewhiskered Mephistopheles of ring toss,
the diabolical vampire of our transcendent ideals.
Every Chuck E. Cheese's erected across the mall-lands of America
is another nail in the coffin of human aspiration
and every hour spent in one takes six months off your life.
No, no, no, it's not a theme restaurant or family amusement center
but a vision of infernal despair enjoined in plastic flames,
the clownish horror of the place is unspeakable,
yet I feel that I must speak of it, for I have been
to the birthday party of Emily, turning five,
the birthday party of Max, turning eight or nine,
of Max again, of David and Doris, of Myrna and Roberto,
I can bear witness to its odors of chocolate milk and floor cleanser,
the formica falsity of its processed cheesefood pseudo-pizza,
its banquet tables arrayed with pitchers of lurid orange soda
and the kids in the arcade room playing air hockey
and whack-a-mole and teaching one another to cheat at skiball
to win a screel of coupons to redeem for tiny, chintzy prizes,
the worst sorts of craftily packaged trash—
stringless army parachute guys, malformed monster finger puppets,
Chinese yo-yos that self-destruct at the flip of a wrist—
a rainbow-colored peepshow designed to entice the youngest among us
to invest their lives in a cycle of competitive consumption
and then the animatronic hoedown commences its banjo jangle,
the hairy rodent orchestra chirring their cymbals on stage
as the gray rat-man emerges from his curtain redolent of mildew,

the incubus, the secret sharer, Chuck E. Cheese himself,
and the baby children scream in dismay and the larger children
gag with disinterest and the parents pay no attention at all
while employees with the fear- and candy-glazed eyeballs
of medium-security inmates stutter their pre-scripted remarks
over a public address system in whose interstitial silences
one may discern the voices of the lost upraised in prayer.

We're having a great day at Chuck E. Cheese—
    Hear us, help us, grant us benison,
Pick up your food at the counter PJ—
    Comfort and guide us, lead us to salvation,
Everyone loves family fun at Chuck E.—
    Bestow the mercies of your blessing
Cheese for your safety wear shoes at all times—
    Upon our souls, we beseech Thee,
Last call for pickup PJ last call—
    Lord of our fathers, almighty God.

The Strangler Fig

Masters, we adore you,
each and all. We praise in you
a generosity of spirit
dreamt of but unknown
among our kind. We are weak
while you are strong,
oak and palm and ruby-
figured gumbolimbo,
the profligate ficus
among whose lordly roots
a toehold may be granted
the needy. *Noblesse
oblige*. In your shadows
we grow dependent.
Let us lean upon you.
Grant us lenience. Let us
gather the crumbs
from your table until
the cords of our temple
are noosed and the pillars
of your hearth cast down
and the manors you
have labored to create,
beloved masters,
yield to the extravagant
vengeance of the risen.

The Florida Anasazi

From above it's a dickie or a verdant tie skewed sideways, banana or schlong, skull of a prehistoric mammal with lower mandible removed and Okeechobee for its eye, a moth-eaten pennant trimmed with blue water, a peninsular thumb bruised a dozen shades of green, emerald fronded jungle and sandy palmetto veldt and the predominant olive dun of once-cleared land reverting to scrub. And from the plane one sees, throughout Florida, titanic etchings upon the ground, quadrants of scarred earth that in their obscure figurative squib resemble the sacred patterns of a primitive mythos, the song lines of aboriginal Australians, or the vast animal figures of the Nazca plateau, or the pictoglyphs of the ancient Anasazi, sun-bleached ochre against canyon wall, fertility symbols and animal visages, banded armadillo and antler flange, mischievous coyote, flute-bowed Kokopeli, so different from the local totems, backhoe, chainsaw, roadkill, stripmall, the alligator-headed figure known to us as The Developer who works his trickery upon the people of the tribe, pilfering communal goods, claiming to produce that which he despoils. This is his signature, this marked and scarred earth, a palimpsest of greed and grand plans gone wrong, a promissory text of spectral subdivisions, roads and cul-de-sacs that never were and yet shall be, premonitory ghost cities rising like the ruins of the Anasazi in reverse, their abandoned pueblos, cliff dwellings slipped into empty rungs on the ladder of need, a civilization as inconspicuous as lichen, vanished after centuries with little to mark its tenure but rock drawings and the shards of earthenware vessels, a midden heap of piñon nuts, a loom shaft carved from juniper wood. The Florida Anasazi aren't here yet, but you can tell they're coming. The mark of their ruin has preceded them, to help them feel at home, and so that we may know them when they arrive.

Mile Marker 73, Lower Matecumbe Key

Seed pods at the tide-line plump as swollen sugar-beans
or a freedom flotilla of Havana cigars crying
sanctuary in the bone flats of soft mud and turtle grass,
wind-driven sargassum Sam jars in glass
to enumerate its scooterized flagellant genera:
seahorse, needlefish, peppermint shrimp, pelagic crab.

Butter-white marl case-hardened to shale
convulses in the prop-fisted, splay-fingered grip
of the stilt-walking, salt-bearing mangrove roots,
tonsils akimbo, elbows loose as ankle bones.

Osprey nest on a telephone pole, pelicans on channel pilings,
flocks of dunlins, whimbrels, gulls,
the solitary cormorant, a family of ring doves.

Happiness unhinge me like the dive of the anhinga!

Seashells, Manasota Key

Abras, augers, arks and angel wings,

bubbles, bittium,
baby's ears,
bleeding teeth,

crenulate nut clams and pointed cingulas,
dogwinkles, diplodons, donax, dosinia,

emarginate emarginula,

fig shells, frog shells, file shells,
flamingo tongue,

geoducks, gem clams, the bittersweet family *Glycymerididae,*

helmets and half-slippers,
hoof shells and horse mussels,

Ischnochitonidae,
Isognomonidae,
Ilynassa obsoleta,

jewel boxes, jingle shells,
kitten's paws,
loras, limas, lucines, lysonias,
murexes, mactras, moon shells, melampuses,

neptune, nerite, glorious neodrillia,

the San Pedro dwarf olive,
Candé's beaded phos,

quarterdecks and quahogs,
razor clams and ribbed miters,

scotch bonnets, shark eyes, slit worms, solarielle,

tritons, turbans, turrets,
tulips, trumpets,
thracias, trivias, tusks and tuns,

unicorns,
venuses and volutes,
wentletraps, wing oysters, lightning whelks,
xenophoridae,
yoldia,

Zebina browniana and *Zirfaea crispata.*

Hemingway Dines on Boiled Shrimp and Beer

I'm the original two-hearted brawler.
I gnaw the scrawny heads from prawns,
pummel those mute, translucent crustaceans,
wingless hummingbirds, salt-water spawned.
As the Catalonians do, I eat the eyes at once.
My brawny palms flatten their mainstays.
I pop the shells with my thumbs, then crunch.

Just watch me as I swagger and sprawl,
spice-mad and sated, then dabble in lager
before I go strolling for stronger waters
down to Sloppy Joe's. My stride as I stagger
shivers the islands, my fingers troll a thousand keys.
My appetite shakes the rock of the nation.
The force of my miction makes the mighty Gulf Stream.

Elizabeth Bishop in the House on White Street

Already almond un-shadow
burns the bougainvillea from sable to shame.

Crinum lilies cry open for

dewfall; pinkly
erogenous
frangipani mimic lacustrine
groves of coral.

Hibiscus,
ixora, night-blooming
jasmine's Socratic dialogue with daylight,

kin to the high tide's
lunar ambrosia.

Many are the gifts
night bestows,
O my flowering beloved!

Pomegranate, sweet
quince,
red-wax ichor of the unripe ackee
suspended in shadow like artificial pears,
teardrops
upon unrustled

verbena. From the minarets of the palms
wild doves summon the faithful.

Xantippe shrills below the sill.

Yellow light assembles its
ziggurat in
air.

Maizel at Shorty's in Kendall

All shift them sugar donuts
been singing to me,
calling to me something crazy in a voice
Dolly Parton'd be proud of—*Maizel, honey,*
eat us up! Like that.
Friendly. Nice and sweet, all
glazed up together in that box, as if they was
happy about being what they
is, surely more than this
jelly-junkie waitress hooked on
Krispy Kremes can say. Halve the moon,
leave a frosted crescent for some other girl.
Maizel, you ain't kidding
no one, honey.
Of a certainty you're gonna eat that yourself,
probably soon's you get these BB-
Q
ribs to them boys at table
sixteen. Nice-looking boys, too.
These days we're getting the,
uh, Cuban mostly,
virtually all what you call Hispanic-speaking.
White folks gone moved up to Broward County, like my
ex. *Maizel, you shut*
your mouth about that man! Sweet Gee-
zus, honey, ain't this ring of sugar gold enough?

The Calusa

For the way the waves of the new-moon water
cross the wide flats of salt-mud and marl
to spill and pool and lap and purl
amongst the roots of the red and black mangroves
there is no word in your wide-traveled tongues.

In our language it was called:

Here is a word for a certain star which is also a flower:
Here is a river-fish, the alligator gar:
Here is a way of speaking of the character of a warrior
unskilled in the ways of village women:

The name of our brother, the great blue heron:
Our brother, who is also our enemy, the hammerhead shark:
A word for the way a greenback turtle lays her eggs:
For the mighty cypress from which we craft our war-canoes:
The name of the wind in the season of pelicans:
A way of saying many whelks or bountiful:
Infant seahorses cradled in brine:
Sand dollar worn through the ear of the chieftain's daughter:
Masks in the forms of crocodiles, dolphins, panthers:

Because our carvers and craftsmen
had not learned to forge Spanish metals
the sacred figures of our artifacts are lost.

Because our priests and storytellers
had not mastered the scribal sorcery of letters

our words vanished with us
like the small round seals rich with fat
we hunted in such numbers to feast upon,

animals whose bones endure in our shell mounds and middens
as the ghost of our language moans through the names of our villages
disfigured by the accents of those
plucked from the torture fires to live amongst us:

Calos, Tanpa, Yobe, Guacata, Escampaba, Mayaimi.

A man has three souls: his shadow,
the reflection he finds waiting to watch in still water,
the flame that dances in the pupil of his eye.
Two perish with him while one abides,
and the name of that eternal spirit is:

Here is a word for a rookery of flamingos and scarlet ibis:
A word for the color of the gulf at first light:

A word for us, the fierce people: Calusa.

The Manatee

Deep sunk in the dreamtime of his terminal coma,
the manatee persists like a vegetative outpatient,
victim of the whirling propellers of impatience
and a buoyantly bovine quiescence gone nova.

Dream deep, brother. Dream long and deep, sister sea-cow.
May millennia of soft tides and seagrass sustain thy sleep
across the dark ages of extinction. May your memory keep
heavy the hearts and hulls of your inheritors. Us, for now.

Trouble with Miami

is the lack of significant galleries & serious theater,
the absence of museums, operas, ballets, symphonies,
a dearth of cultural infrastructure so profound

that the only local institution worth its salt is the ocean,

that watching the beautiful women on the beach
with bodies cast from bronze & soft lobed chrome
may be our best shot at real enlightenment,

their formal aspects comprise our artistic endowment,
their lubricity constitutes our esthetic nourishment,

hard candy loaves & fishes,

a sculpture garden of erotic possibility
displayed in postures of wicked amusement
like wild palms abandoned to wind and solar decay,

and I am a happily married man
who sunburns easily.

At the Royal Palm Barbershop

FOR MICHAEL COLLIER

At the Royal Palm Barbershop I am hailed by bells,
I am called "young fellow,"
I reside within the nautilus chambers of memory.

At the Royal Palm Barbershop we peruse the local papers
in rattan chairs, chew upon unlit El Productos,
jig the palomino tassels of our loafers while we wait;

the heavy pedestal ballglass ashtrays carol the tunes of yesteryear,
anachronistic as barroom cuspidors, as the blue
medicinal vials of Aqua Velva

encrypted in lost codes of tonic
and dust. *The do's
and don'ts of handsome hair* adorn the paneled walls,

travel posters bespeaking identity,
Jerusalem and Havana, Miami Beach;
three flags for Cuba, Israel, and the U.S. of A.

At the Royal Palm Barbershop there is no extra charge for "Roffler
    Styling."
At the Royal Palm Barbershop
I surrender to the ritual ministrations of compassion:

lave and salve,
adoration of the straight razor,
the laying on of hands.

The scissor clip behind an ear keys the echolocation of bats,
nosings of a mole, the fruit rat
upon his twilight vigil. At the Royal Palm Barbershop

Kenny displays his diploma from the College of Coiffure,
his specialty the Sculpture Kut,
a practice he works on the weak-willed or unwary;

the man on the next chair appears to have drowned
within a turban of hot towels and lather,
toes unholy as bloated otters in tiny buckets of oiled water.

At the Royal Palm Barbershop I am whisked and talced,
I pledge again my allegiance to this world,
I plight my troth to the faithful arms of the sunlight,

shorn of the weight of the present,
unburdened of the past,
little changed and yet renewed. (O the broom sings,

the broom sings
of its bondage, curled and wizened,
as you rise to pay.)

At the Royal Palm Barbershop you can crunch
Kiwanis gumballs on your way out the door,
click the tutti-frutti castanets of chiclets for a nickel,

crack your enamel on a Jewish Fund jawbreaker
or toss a bill for *Hermanos al Rescate*
as you wave so long to Joseph, Eddie, Alex, Ken.

At the Royal Palm Barbershop
we are all brothers,
and saved.

The Miami Beach Holocaust Memorial

A great green hand reaches up to the Florida sky.
Circled in palms, ringed by bowers of white bougainvillea,
its flesh is wrought of mellifluous iron, color
of olive leaves, from which emerge a human multitude
transfigured to forms of tortured supplication,
blind wraiths ascending to grace amid the graven
numerals of the death camps and the lily pond
reflecting clouds like faces cast down in silent vigil.
From his grandmother Sam has learned that these
are people "climbing away from their troubles,"
a formula that quiets without satisfying his curiosity,
piqued daily, en route to the grocery store,
by this incongruous vision across from the golf course,
and I'm glad he isn't with me today, stuck behind tour buses
unleashing lines of mourners come to honor
some black anniversary, elders grim
with the rectitude of their homburgs, a coterie
of teenagers from the high school waving placards
proclaiming *Never Forget* and *Never Again,*
slogans predicated upon an immemorial desire
to believe in the perfectibility of humankind
even in the face of such witness to our monstrosity
as the testimonial obelisk of horrors that is
history. Brick upon brick, blueprint after blueprint,
so the Grand Edifice of Civilization takes shape,
Xanadu abandoned in favor of prison ramparts,
blind walls to guard us from that most savage enemy,
he that abideth within, and you are welcome
to whatever degree of optimism you feel justified

in the efficacy of such constructs to protect us
from ourselves, as witness Odysseus' horse at Troy,
Joshua's horn at Jericho. When Hadrian's Wall
went up the Scots came down from the hills
to attack the Roman legions naked,
smeared with tallow, keening wildly in the snow.
Even the Great Wall of China could not keep
the Mongols at bay forever. So have we advanced,
horde upon horde, so surmounted wall after
wall after wall. Flood upon fresh flood,
the tide of blood deepens and renews itself,
generation unto generation, the will to remember
overthrown by the flesh's obligation to forget,
to erect its temple on the scorched foundation of the old,
to clean the slate and chalk a new testament
to become a ghostly palimpsest for future ages.
Thus we recall the Provençal only for their troubadours,
the Olmecs for astronomy and the fanged god of tropical rain.
We remember Lucy because the australopithecines
walked upright and killed efficiently,
and we have survived them in like manner,
killing and being killed, strong in a world of strength,
and even when they have outlived their usefulness
we cannot disregard the deep structures
of our inheritance, the genetic press recycling its type,
guanine, adenine, thymine, cytosine,
enzymes comprising a map of the species,

instructions for assembly in a language of universal simplicity
as with the diagrams that accompany architect's lamps
or Scandinavian furniture, G A T C, four letters
we share with chimps and whales and lilies
and phytoplankton, all living matter descended
from the original lucky molecule. Which is to say:
evolution. Which is not to say: progress.
This is what I'd like to say to Sam, to tell him
without having to tell him, though I would never
indulge the false bravery to spill this bitter cup
into a child's ear. Someday Sam's children,
the children of my childrens' children, however many times
removed, will remember us, dimly and inaccurately,
for the mythic splendor of our golden arches,
as they peer forth from places of hiding in the ghettos
or scrublands of whatever cities or deserts remain,
as they are hunted down, one by one, whether
for the red hair of the Celts still clinging to their forearms
or the life-force of the Jews bequeathed them by Elizabeth
or the vestigial memory of some as yet undreamed
category of violent distinction and hatred.
Up from the swamplands and avenues of Florida,
and the edenic faiths and faces of Florida,
and the towers that spring from the fertile sands of Florida,
and the flowers that predate the magic cities of Florida,
a great green hand ascends toward the heavens.
People have assembled around it in the sunshine.

They are singing or they are weeping. They are
fingering its wrist, crowding its tower of stairs to a standstill.
They are climbing away from their troubles,
crying out. They are green and floral. They are metal.
They are ash. They are flesh. They are us.

Late February, Miami Beach

All morning the woodpecker drills holes in the oranges
left to rot upon the highest limbs;
barbarous jays gather twigs to build a nest
in the barren live oak,
in the wishbone branches of the royal poinciana,
in the pollen-spiked sponge of a blossoming mango tree.

Already the days bear within them the seed
of what is to come—flowers
born at dawn to perish in the furnace of mid-afternoon.

Thus the gardenia hoards its fragrance for nightfall.
Thus jasmine husbands its pearls until dusk.

After dinner I see the face of my father
looking back at me from the kitchen window,
secretive, aquiline, ferreting out one chocolate cookie,
one swig of milk from the carton as the baby is put to bed,
this small hunger nurtured like an orchid,
indulged precisely, in a prism of refractive solitude.

Beyond the glass the moon in its reflected glory
shepherds clouds off the Atlantic on a trade wind
scented by blossoms of excruciating beauty.

The Zebra Longwing

Forty years I've waited,
uncomprehending,
for these winter nights
when the butterflies
fold themselves like paper cranes
to sleep in the dangling
roots of the orchids
boxed and hung
from the live oak tree.
How many there are.
Six. Eight. Eleven.
When I mist the spikes
and blossoms by moonlight
they stir but do not wake,
antennaed and dreaming
of passionflower
nectar. Never before
have they gifted us
in like manner, never before
have they stilled their flight
in our garden. Wings
have borne them away
from the silk
of the past as surely
as some merciful wind
has delivered us
to an anchorage of such
abundant grace,

Elizabeth. All my life
I have searched, without knowing it,
for this moment.

Florida

If they'd had a spark of wit or vision
it would be known today as Cloudiana,
in honor of the mighty Alps and Andes
assembled and cast westward as rain
and thunder each and every afternoon.

If they'd understood the grave
solemnity of the sublime
it would be named for the great blue heron:

for longevity, the alligator;
for tenacity, the mosquito;
for absurdity, the landcrab.

If they had any sense
of history
it would be called Landgrab,

it would be called Exploitatiania,

for the bulldozed banyans,
lost cathedrals of mahogany and cypress,
savannas of sawgrass and sabal palm,
mangroves toiling to anchor their buttresses,
knitting and mending the watery verge.

Beautiful and useless, flowers
bloom and die

in every season here, their colors dissemble,
soft corpses underfoot.

If there was any justice in this world
it would be named
Mangrovia.

THREE

THE FLORIDA POEM

The Florida Poem

Let me start by saying this
about Florida.
About the history of Florida, the proud beginnings
of Florida, proud and noble begin-
ings/genesis/roots/traditions, about the
histo—about the mythic identity
of Florida, its sun-loving soul, its vital essence,
vegetable essence,
its profound and mythic something,
it's something.
Let me start
again: organ swell, diapason,
incant the appropriate invocation.
Hear me now, o Floridian muse!
Sing through me, o native goddess, o sacred orange
blossom nymph, o Weeki Wachee naiad,
o Minnie, o Daisy,
o dappled condominium queen,
o dryad of the fairway and practice green, o
my, oh my, o one more
try. Flo-
ri-
da. Florrr
rrida!
Florida: it's here!
Florida: it's here and it's for sale!
Florida: it's neat, in a weird way!
Florida: Fuckin' Fantastic!
This would be my official suggestion for a new state motto,

certainly not something the Legislature
is likely to consider
an appropriate means of promoting
our fabulous natural resources and dynamic
growth potential. Their idea of useful
is another ladle of lard from the old coffee can
of boosterism and bacon fat,
something like—Florida:
shelter your profits in the sunshine state!
Florida: wreak your retiree havoc here!
Florida: just come on down
and exploit it!
Ah, but I digress. The point
was to buy into Florida, not to sell it again,
and anyway when it comes to sloganeering
I'm no match for the marketers
and technocrats and mousketeer apparatchiks
industriously zoning and rezoning the commonwealth,
though I still believe the perfect tag-line is waiting
to be coined, the perfect come-on
for a place whose history begins and ends
with a sales pitch,
a shill, a wink and a nudge
and a can of green paint to valorize the scrublands
and scorched savannas peddled to unwary out-of-towners,
beginning with Ponce de León himself,
who sold an expedition of greed and self-gratification
as a mystical quest for a Fountain of Youth which,
had it existed, would by now

have been hijacked as symbolic centerpiece
for some cookie-cutter cluster
of master-planned contemporary custom home communities
and then bled dry with the vanishing aquifers
until the riddled earth itself surrendered
and every beloved one of those
houses and lap pools and riding mowers and mortgage balloons
vanished into the maw of the newly rechristened
Sinkhole of Youth. Luckily,
this tragic scenario was averted by the Calusa,
who recognized at a glance the vehicle of their annihilation
and so dispatched unhappy Ponce with an arrow
dipped in manchineel sap,
and by the unfortunate fact that there was no miraculous
resuscitative font but merely the false
promise of loot to lure
the conquistadors into this land of illusions,
though I myself have more than once
been enticed to swim in the icy oasis of DeLeon Springs,
and have eaten at the remarkable restaurant
reputedly housed in an old Spanish mill
where they grind still the wheat
to mix the batter you pool and flip on a griddle
in the middle of your very own table.
Pancakes!
Pancakes and alligators and paddleboats and ruins
of vanished conquerors vanquished
in their turn. It's one of my favorite places in the state,
not merely for the flapjacks and historical ironies

but for the chaste fact of its beauty,
its palmettos and live oaks and the liquid upwelling
of subterranean rivers that have underlain this peninsula
for millennia, waters we are even now
exhausting but which endure,
which yet remain to nourish and sustain us,
a consolation
which must become the fountain
for any communal future we might dare imagine,
source and wellspring of the hope
and courage it will take
to fight for the preservation of what is good
against the diverse and relentless forces of destruction
loosed upon this flower-drunk relic
of the original garden,
mere vestige perhaps
of the trackless cornucopia of the Calusa,
but at least it is a vestige
of paradise.
Now this, in all fairness, is not
a purely local issue
in the way that, say, alligators scarfing pet poodles is.
Paradisal vestiges could serve as synonym
for reality as we know it,
a working definition of the human condition,
shorthand for the universality of our postlapsarian inheritance,
the ways in which the world we inhabit
survives as an embodiment of previous and equally viable
worlds, civilizations, epochs, reigns,

as even the galactic clouds where stars are conceived
like Moorish idols in a crucible of swan-light
riven by gestures of radiant indigo
themselves refract the luminous matter of some previous
inchoate and irrecoverable dawn.
I refer, of course, to the past, the sunken treasure fleet
of time gone, lost realm of anchor chains
fixed in coral, pearls returned
to the forge of their origin, cannons and amphorae
that beckon us not so much for what they are or were
as for what they represent, as His Excellency
Juan Ponce de León
represents the beginning
of the end
for a regime with roots
descending unbroken twelve thousand years
to the Pleistocene, a mosaic
of indigenous cultures ripped from the walls
by the wind of European arrival
in scarce two centuries. And then the walls demolished.
And the temple razed and burned.
Not that Ponce in any literal way discovered the place,
not even euphemistically, not even Eurocentrically,
it being known to Cuban slavers a dozen years
before he made landfall,
April 2nd, 1513,
prior to which moment he had been famous primarily
for his rapacious and impecunious service
as Royal Governor of Puerto Rico,

which *Isla del Encanto* he had Most Fittingly
Conquered and Enslaved in the name of his Majesty,
and of Our Lord, Jesus Christus,
and we would certainly no longer remember him
except for the business about the Fountain of Youth,
and his nominal status as founder of Florida,
and the lingering controversy as to why he named it as he did.
Well, for one thing it sounds better in Spanish,
elegant and florid, peaks and valleys,
a far cry from that flat, Americanized dogbite: Flrda.
Also it was Easter, *Pascua Florída,*
when the land bloomed
heavy with flowers and Catholic piety
and so the name was struck like a two-faced doubloon,
duly minted, sealed, bestowed,
and stuck: *La Florída.*
Island of Flowers.
The Beflowered Land.
Flowervania.
It doesn't really translate
but you'd know it by the odor of jasmine
and rain-drenched earth, fat worms in warm puddles,
fronds and petals in riotous abandon,
a continent of elastic green fecundity looming
floral and renascent. And after de León another fifty years
of Spaniards shipwrecked on the rock of the unreal,
noble adventurers eighty-sixed at the hands of intransigent nature
or the primitive, soon to vanish *indios*—
Pánfilo de Narváez, Tristán de Luna y Arellano,

so read their sandy and melodious epitaphs,
most famously that of Hernando de Soto, "the never-
conquered cavalier," veteran of the egg-scrambling *entrada*
that fried the Incas up in one big
genocidal omelet, mighty de Soto whose watchword
was gold—*Where is the gold? Where are
the mountains?*—who marched north with 500 soldiers
through swamps and plains and forests, north
the length of a state with a heart like a giant stalk of celery,
mocked by the clouds that are the actual mountains
of this place, no more than a rumor
of rain on the horizon,
a horizon of expectations no literal horizon could meet,
burning the villages of the Indians who fled
at word of his approach, palm-thatched huts
and cypress palisades and plantings
of squash and pumpkins trampled by the horses,
fields of green corn in flames,
screams of the dazed or captured peoples,
a people not hard to see as not people,
daughter of the *cacique*
thrown to the wardogs and torn asunder,
others impaled on spikes,
others burned alive,
the *cacique* himself with nose cut off, and ears,
by Sword of mine own Hand, for his Impertinence,
for Refusal to Tell the Location of the Gold most surely Abounding
in That Land, or the next kingdom north, or the next
beyond that—Ocale, Potano, Napituca

where he massacred hundreds for like misbehavior,
Iniahica now Tallahassee, then north again
beyond the state line and the bounds of this poem—*where
is the gold?*—north as far as Carolina
and west almost to Texas, dying at last
of fever and despair near the banks of the Mississippi
he is wrongly said to have discovered,
his corpse dispatched to the great river's mercy
under cover of darkness so as to keep hidden from the enemies
surrounding his starving and diminished army—
tribes already incubating
the germs
that would extinguish Mississippian
civilization—the fact
of his mortality.
He was no god, de Soto.
He was ours
and we cannot disclaim him.
So we must seek to understand his desire
to sow devastation as the staple
crop of the republic. Was he insane?
Or just being sensible?
Equipped as for war one does not arrive uninvited
in the land of another folk simply
to bake cupcakes. In this regard the Indians were nothing
but grain crushed in the mill of his merciless errand,
the gears of profit, yes,
of alienated desire, greed beyond limitation,
but that machine could not function without the grease

of human industry, the oil of human nature,
the psychology that drives armies of men
across a blood-engirdled globe
even now. And these Indians, however easily romanticized,
were similarly human, familiar with power and avarice,
plagued by incessant warfare,
only their systems were simpler and less efficient,
they had evolved no complex structures
or technologies of destruction,
they created no lasting monuments, built no highways
of nail salons and auto parts discount stores,
fashioned no industrial parks beyond sand mounds and shell middens
and so their ten-thousand-year tenure has been erased
with barely a ripple in the sawgrass
to betray it. So much
for the Calusa. So much for the Appalachee,
the Tequesta, the Jororo, the Aís.
So much for the Spanish.
They founded Saint Augustine and later Pensacola,
evicted the French, enslaved the locals,
their missions subsisted for a century among the Timucua
before succumbing to disease, exhaustion
and colonial depredations. Next
the English took a turn, the Spanish once more,
the English again—Florida danced at heel
like a dog with many masters,
like a lady finger soaked in brine, pretty to look at
but who would deign to banquet
on sodden cookies when the grand buffet of colonialism

groaned with bullion and silver plate?—
until at last Andrew Jackson bought the whole place
for five million dollars and a solemn promise
to relinquish all future American
claims to Texas.
Hmm.
By the time the deal was done
it was 1821. A new
century, a new society, a new destiny
shivering the tracks like a clamorous locomotive,
whirling dynamo of energy and change!
Actually, not much happened in Florida in the 19th century.
It drifted along, balmily somnolent,
a backwater of boll weevils and palmetto cowboys,
hardly less a colony for davening
to a new set of stars
and stripes. The town of Cowford
was renamed Jacksonville, to honor Old Hickory
and in udder disregard
for the sentiments of the cows;
steamships appeared, opening the interior to navigation
and thereby requiring the removal of the last, unwelcome indigenes;
so came the Seminole Wars, forty years
of episodic guerrilla campaigns that made of the U.S. Army
a laughingstock for its cowardice, sloth and ineptitude,
culminating in the infamous capture of Osceola
under flag of truce,
a low point in our military annals,
to say the least. And then

the big tamale,
the Civil War, Florida
on the wrong side, per usual,
mandarin in its certitude
of chattel ownership and the patent inhumanity
of its African constituency. Little drama
at the siege of Pensacola, the battle of Olustee;
Florida had no Shiloh, no Gettysburg or Appomattox,
no Valley Forge, no Alamo
except the rental cars,
no Plymouth Rock or Liberty Bell or even Monticello—
Florida is bereft of mythic infrastructure,
symbolically impoverished,
its hallowed grounds are golf courses,
its great cathedrals malls and theme parks,
its founding fathers rank profiteers,
its poets and sages the hucksters and boosters
who banged the drums of development at any cost.
Not from the head of Zeus
but of Henry Flagler
have we sprung. "That Government
will be most highly esteemed
that gives the greatest protection
to individual and industrial enterprises at the least cost
to the taxpayers," said Governor George F. Drew,
an unusually frank equation for corporate entitlement
at the expense of civic need, no huge surprise
in a state whose political legacy
is the legislative equivalent of Osceola's ambush,

a daisy-chain scissored from sweetheart bills and broken treaties
in the image of old Jim Crow
crowned with paper shackles riding a piebald mule.
What the governor meant was
come and get it,
tear it
down, rip it up,
mill it for lumber, boil it for turpentine,
orchard it for oranges or pit-mine it for phosphates,
shoot it for hides or skins or quills
or fun, can it for soup,
pack it, ship it, fish it to the verge
of fishlessness, suck
the candy
from this cane as best you can
before the sugar runs dry,
a mindset of witless and exploitative destruction
embraced not only by gilded tycoons
but by hunters and gatherers of every stripe,
as witness those original tourists riding paddlewheel steamers
up primordial rivers in an orgy of gunfire at whatever
moved and much that did not,
or the entrepreneurial collectors who scoured the Everglades
for the colorful shells of tree snails, each
islandlike hammock of mahogany and gumbolimbo
harboring a uniquely patterned subspecies,
and after finding some dozen or hundred
they would torch to barren rock each irreplaceable islet,
each evolutionarily distinctive micro-environment,

thereby assuring the extinction of that type
and maximizing the value
of their specimens. Which brings us
stumbling into the streamlined stage-lights of modernity
with its attendant surfeit of the all-but-miraculous,
sound and fury befitting a century of marvels
and yet for all the hubbub not much
really happened in the last one hundred years either.
Not much has ever happened in Florida, to tell the truth.
Another way of conceiving our history
would be to admit up front
that from de León's very first sand-cast heel-print
to the final toe-touch of Neil Armstrong's silver space-age booties
bound from Cape Canaveral for a sea of lunar dust
not a single human footfall within these soggy confines
could dare assert any claim to lasting, world-historical import.
Another way of conceiving this poem would be
to acknowledge that all of this—
16, 17, 18, 19,
even our lovingly eulogized 20th century—
comprises five hundred years of humid inconsequence,
prologue to a long-deferred moment of reckoning,
an invoice of accountability come due at last,
now that it is no longer possible
to erase what has come before us and begin anew,
now that the ruined orchard rejects our claim of usufruct,
now that fifteen million must drink from one spigot
and Florida's crucible of self-definition
is at hand,

its coming-out party, its *quinces,*
the dawning
of its Immortal Metal Age,
though who but an alchemist would dare predict
whether Gold or Lead it shall be? O
the future, the future,
the future,
o!
Frankly,
it scares the hell out of me.
Yes, I know that our very weaknesses might
become a source of unsuspected strength,
that a lack of iconic identity allows us the chance
to fashion unfettered a society of diverse and fluid beauty
unlike any ever known, of course,
after all I'm an optimist,
a romantic, a believer but also
a skeptic and so
fated to perform the calculus of the probable
and weep at our stupidity
carried forward through the steam tables and logarithms
of a new millennium, where already the ocean
at whose hem we kneel in oiled worship
rises to consume us incrementally,
to reclaim a rebel province for the holy empire of salt,
and even if Florida does not believe in history
it cannot help but believe
in the tide, and the tide for its part is

a compelling historian. And yet, all it takes
is a day at the beach
to see the slate scrubbed clean
and scribbled anew
by the beautiful coquinas, to witness
the laws of hydraulics rendered moot by the munificent
tranquillity of their variegated colonies
thriving amid the chaos of wave-break and overwash.
All it takes is a *cafécito* in the Miami airport,
five minutes at the brushed aluminum lunch counter
to realize that an entire hemisphere of human possibility
is wobbling toward us
upon an axis whose orbit no astral mathematics
could possibly model. All it takes is a summer afternoon
floating the pellucid Ichetucknee River
to plumb the dragonfly's eye
of its fluvial essence
and recognize how much has been lost since William Bartram's day
and yet how much of such elemental loveliness
is left. One immersion is all you need
to be born into such faith,
one brushstroke to be watermarked,
indelibly graven—one glance
toward that pool of azure light through the trees ahead—
nomad opal drenched in nectar!—
to understand that the Fountain of Youth does exist, it always has,
our chronic myopia must be reckoned a token
of the years lost deciphering Ye Olde Spanish Maps,

because they too could never find what swam
before their eyes, and like them we have been blinded
by larcenous intentions, by the vanity of mastery,
by our fear at being labeled traffickers
in utopian fantasies,
though it is not in actuality some fairy-tale
geyser of childish enchantment or escape from the real
but a reservoir of the profound,
an oasis of the sacred,
an emblem of solace and renewal
in a difficult world. A simple leap is enough
to know the invigoration of that embrace, visceral opulence
of an element so clear each grain of sand
sings forth, each bordering leaf of oak or heliconia,
each minnow or sunfish in the mineral wicker-work,
one jump, one plunge
toward the crevice of rifted limestone
wherefrom the earth pours forth
its liquid gift,
glorying in the acids and sunlight of motion
as you stretch to reach the ungraspable,
striving forward,
borne back, held suspended
within its invisible pulse—austere, enigmatic, elastic—
like the votive force of time we push against
and are scoured and scourged
and washed clean by, what it's like
to be alive, how
it flows, not from past to present or present to future

but from source to vanishing, from source
to vanishing to source,
which would be an even better way
of conceiving this poem, to reverse its polarity,
invert the pyramid of chronology
and retreat from the saw-buzz of highrise cranes
constructing the moment, draw back
toward the silted and the half-dim, past Spanish moss
and dangling chads, Apollo in flames,
past Arthur Godfrey's ukulele,
past railroad barons and the Green Cross Republic,
slaves and zealots and buccaneers,
past the Calusa and the Creek moving south
to supplant them, past the Okeechobee mound-builders,
past the Weeden Island people,
the unnamed people,
past the Hopewellian and the Archaic
to the fringe of the Holocene when they came,
in the hoar weather of early spring,
across Beringia and down coast or canyon
or glaciated sluiceway into the open plains of the continent,
human beings, clans and bands of paleo-Indians
trailing the great herds through the dying winter of the megafaunal age,
crossing somehow the mountains and steppes and rivers,
finding their way to the brine tide of the gulf,
continental shelf rich with shellfish,
sharks and rays in the shallows, sea turtles
overturned and butchered and eaten among the dunes,
following the coastline as it bent

to the east and southward
toward this terminal, scallop-backed cul-de-sac,
higher and drier then, arid peninsula
of grasslands and brushy savannas that meant
good hunting of glyptodonts, ground sloths, giant tortoises,
peccary and jaguar, horse and condor,
mastodons and camelids and bison, varieties of horned stock
unknown to us these millennia past
gathered at muddy pools and waterholes,
a place beyond which there was no further passage,
a place where some would turn again
to the north, some double back west and away, gone,
a place where, after hesitating,
after testing the air for what they most depended on,
some few among them
moved cautiously forward and so became
the first of our kind to enter
into Florida,
and stooped at the edge
of a spring among rushes and tall sedge,
touching knee to muddy verge
to cup a palm
and find that it was fresh and thus
a livable land,
a place of mutable possibility, tabula rasa,
a place in which to fashion
from the mortar of water and sunshine
a life, now

as on that day so long ago,
that unmarked and immemorial day,
the first day
of our existence,
today.

Claremont Courier

CAMPBELL McGRATH's previous collections are *Capitalism, American Noise, Spring Comes to Chicago,* and *Road Atlas.* His awards include the Kingsley Tufts Prize and fellowships from the Guggenheim and MacArthur Foundations. He teaches in the creative writing program at Florida International University in Miami.

Printed in the USA
CPSIA information can be obtained
at www.ICGtesting.com
LVHW030839101223
766054LV00007B/49